OUR LADY'S TUMBLER

by the same author

*

THIS WAY TO THE TOMB
THE MONGREL AND OTHER POEMS
STRATTON

*

JOURNAL OF A HUSBANDMAN
HOME-MADE HOME

OUR
LADY'S
TUMBLER

Ronald Duncan

FABER & FABER LIMITED

24 Russell Square

London

First published in mcmli
by Faber and Faber Limited
24 Russell Square London W.C.1
Printed in Great Britain by
Latimer Trend & Co Ltd Plymouth

This play was commissioned by the Salisbury and District Society of Arts as part of the celebrations for the Festival of Britain. It was first performed in Salisbury Cathedral on the fifth of June mcml.

The music for this play was composed by Mr. Arthur Oldham. The score is obtainable from Messrs. Boosey & Hawkes Ltd., 295 Regent Street, London, W.1. The decor for the original production was by Cecil Beaton.

Inquiries concerning the performing rights should be addressed to Margery Vosper Ltd., 32 Shaftesbury Avenue, London, W.1.

Es vies des anciens peres
La on sont bones les materes
Nos raconte on d'un examplel;
Jo ne di mie c'alsi bel
N'ait on oi par maintes fois
Mais cil n'est pas si en desfois
Ne face bien a raconter
Or vos voil dire et aconter
D'un menestrel que li avint. . . .

"DEL TUMBEOR NOSTRE DAME",
ANONYMOUS FRENCH TWELFTH
CENTURY. TEXT TAKEN FROM
ARTICLE BY WILHELM FOERSTER
IN "ROMANIA" (LIBRAIRE A.
FRANK. PARIS 1873)

CHARACTERS

FATHER MARCELLUS	an abbot
BROTHER SEBASTIAN	a poet
BROTHER JUSTIN	a composer
BROTHER GREGORY	a gardener
BROTHER ANDREW	a novice

The scene is set in a chapel. The action takes place before a statue of the Blessed Virgin. The period is not specified.

The play is in one act and is so designed that, if necessary, it may be performed in a church or hall without a stage or house curtain. The statue is the only essential property.

OUR LADY'S TUMBLER

Before the statue of the Blessed Virgin. To the right, Brother Sebastian is seen, seated on a step. He is writing, the paper is held on his knee, a broom beside him.

A mixed choir sing (off)

HYMN OF DEDICATION

If love is made of words,
    Who can love more than I?
If love is all self-love,
    Who's more beloved than I?

If love is made of faith,
    Who can love less than I?
If love is to submit,
    Who's less beloved than I?

If love is made of tears,
    Who could love more than she?
If love is to betray,
    Who was beloved as He?

Oh may my fickle heart
    Be faithful to my soul;
Deceiving jealous Death,
    Betray my life to Thee.

ARIA *(Tenor solo off)*

O Virgin Mother,
    Your arms were made a cradle,
And that cradle
    was for Him.
        Your care was as gentle,
                gentle as the candle
Lighting the low stable;
        that high throne at His birth.

O Virgin Mother,
    Your heart was made for sorrow,
And that sorrow
    was for Him.
        Your grief was as heavy,
                heavy as the thunder
Rending the high hill to
        that valley of His death.

O Virgin Mother,
    Your lips were made for gladness,
And that gladness
    was for Him.
        Your smile was as happy,
                happy as His Spirit
Leaving the sepulchre,
        that palace as He rose.

O Virgin Mother,
    Your eyes were made for pity,
And that pity
    is for Man.

Your love is as gracious,

gracious as a river

Flowing through this desert,

this desert which is Man.

BROTHER SEBASTIAN

(reading his composition over to himself)

'He stands as a beggar, yet it is I who am blind,
  Nor does he seek for alms, but to give me sight;
For my sin is self-love and all my days are darker than the
    night. . . .'

That's clumsy! . . . I don't like the inversion: 'nor does he seek
    for alms'.
It's terribly clumsy. . . .
Let's try: 'He does not seek for alms but to give me sight.'
Yes, that's clearer and has got rid of that inversion.
Now how does it run?
'He stands as a beggar, yet it is I who am blind,
  He does not seek for alms but to give me sight;
For my sin is self-love and all my days are darker than the
    night.'
Still not right. The last line stumbles like a centipede that's
out of step.
'For my sin is self-love . . .' another inversion—that's the worst
    of knowing too much Latin;
Must alter that, somehow. . . .

*(Brother Andrew comes in carrying a pail. He starts to scrub the aisle,
    and seems unaware of Brother Sebastian's presence)*
'For my sin is self-love' . . . No: 'for self-love is my sin.'

12

BROTHER ANDREW

(to himself as he noisily pushes his pail about)

'Amo, amas, amat,
 Amamus, amatis *(pause)* amant.'
'amabo, amabis, amabit,
 amabimus, amabitis . . . *(pause)*

BROTHER SEBASTIAN

'For self-love's my sin'
No, 'For my eyes are blind with self-love'—yes, that's better.

BROTHER ANDREW

'Amabo, amabis, amabit,
amabimus, amabitis . . . *(pause, then almost proudly)* amabint!'

BROTHER SEBASTIAN

(correcting him without looking up)

'Bunt.'

BROTHER ANDREW

'Amabunt.'

BROTHER SEBASTIAN

'For my eyes are blind with self-love and my days are darker
    than the night.'
That's worse. Now it sounds as if that centipede's got gout!

BROTHER ANDREW

'Amabam, amabas, amabat,
amabamus, amabatis, ama . . . *(pause)*

13

'Bant.'

'For my eyes are blind with self-love and all my days are night.'

BROTHER ANDREW

(*moving his pail as emphasis*)

'Amabant.'

BROTHER SEBASTIAN

'He stands as a beggar;
  He does not seek for alms, but to give me sight;
For my eyes are blind with self-love and all my days are night.
Night that is darker than darkness
      night that . . .'

BROTHER ANDREW

'Amavi, amavisti, amavit,
amavimus . . .

BROTHER SEBASTIAN

Do you mind?

BROTHER ANDREW

'Ssh . . . 'amavimus, amavistis'

BROTHER SEBASTIAN

Brother Andrew . . .

BROTHER ANDREW

Yes?

BROTHER SEBASTIAN

Do you mind? . . .

BROTHER ANDREW

What?

14

BROTHER SEBASTIAN

Oh, nothing. I thought perhaps I was interrupting you.
Are you sure I'm not disturbing you or preventing you from
    concentrating?

BROTHER ANDREW

No, not at all, Brother Sebastian.
I don't mind in the least.

BROTHER SEBASTIAN

Indeed, that's very good of you.

BROTHER ANDREW

Not at all. I'm used to working with people watching me.

BROTHER SEBASTIAN

Are you? Why, of course—I was forgetting.
But you see, Brother Andrew, I am not so fortunate:
I lack your professional experience . . .
So do you mind not imitating a parrot,
And taking your amo amas amat elsewhere,
So that I get on with my work?

BROTHER ANDREW

I'm sorry. I didn't know you were doing anything.
I thought you were just sitting down.

BROTHER SEBASTIAN

So I am 'just sitting down' . . .
Why must everyone, especially in a monastery,
assume that unless you've got a pail in one hand
and a hammer in the other—you're not doing anything?
As a matter of fact, I was thinking.

BROTHER ANDREW

Why, have you lost something?

BROTHER SEBASTIAN

Do I look as if I have? . . .
Ah, I see what you mean . . . dear Brother Andrew.
No, I've not lost anything; I was just thinking of something
I've never had—
well, never long enough to lose.

BROTHER ANDREW

Yes, good money is very hard to come by, isn't it?

BROTHER SEBASTIAN

Is it?

BROTHER ANDREW

Well, it was—
I can't get used to the fact that I don't need it no more . . .

BROTHER SEBASTIAN

If you must know:
I was trying to finish a poem
which I've been trying to write
with a broom in one hand and . . .

BROTHER ANDREW

You made it up yourself?
I wish I could write poetry.

BROTHER SEBASTIAN

Don't you?
I have yet to meet anybody who doesn't.

The reason why nobody reads poetry to-day is:
Everybody's too busy writing it.
You should—it's most relaxing.

BROTHER ANDREW

No, I can never find a rime,
But I did once make up a song, a sort of a ballad . . .

BROTHER SEBASTIAN

What a pity! I hoped you were unique.

BROTHER ANDREW

What's your poem about?

BROTHER SEBASTIAN

It's a canzone.

BROTHER ANDREW

Is it in Latin?

BROTHER SEBASTIAN

No, though that would have been easier.

BROTHER ANDREW

What's it called?

BROTHER SEBASTIAN

'A Prayer for Our Lady's Intercession'.
I've written it for the Celebration.

BROTHER ANDREW

What celebration?

B   17

BROTHER SEBASTIAN

This evening's, of course.
I shall recite my poem before the statue,
As an offering to Our Lady.

BROTHER ANDREW

She'll like that.
Do you always read your poems to her?

BROTHER SEBASTIAN

No, of course not.
Don't you know what day it is? Can't you read the calendar?

BROTHER ANDREW

No, I can't make Latin out yet.

BROTHER SEBASTIAN

But hasn't anybody told you?
Don't you know why you're giving the floor an extra scrub?
And why I'm sweeping with one hand and writing with the
   other?

BROTHER ANDREW

To brighten the place up, I suppose.

BROTHER SEBASTIAN

Yes, because to-day happens to be
The feast day of the Blessed Virgin.

BROTHER ANDREW

And your poem's a sort of birthday present?

18

BROTHER SEBASTIAN

One of three offerings.

BROTHER ANDREW

(*to statue*)

Nobody told me it was your birthday,
Or I'd have done something too.

BROTHER SEBASTIAN

Never mind, Brother Andrew, you can watch with the others.
The chapel will soon be full—
Everybody in the village will be here,
And people come from miles around
    to see whether the statue will move.

BROTHER ANDREW

Does she really?

BROTHER SEBASTIAN

Don't you know? I thought everybody knew.
It's a legend: when the perfect offering is made, the statue will
    make a sign.

BROTHER ANDREW

(*to statue*)

You see, I wasn't here last year. And nobody told me.
So I haven't got you anything.

BROTHER SEBASTIAN

(*interested and touched by Brother Andrew's simplicity*)

Brother Andrew, tell me what made you become a novice?

19

BROTHER ANDREW

My heart.

BROTHER SEBASTIAN

You mean, you had a vocation?

BROTHER ANDREW

Yes, my heart used to go pit-a-pat
Whenever I did my . . .
Whenever I did anything vigorous.

BROTHER SEBASTIAN

Ah, palpitations . . .

BROTHER ANDREW

That's it; so I had to stop . . .
so I had to give the profession up
right in the middle of the season.
Three years next Christmas it'll be.

BROTHER SEBASTIAN

I understand: a vacation more than a vocation . . .
But what made you become a novice?
Couldn't you have retired to a little farm or . . .

BROTHER ANDREW

It wasn't because I hadn't any money, don't think that.
But I was sort of lonely, you see
—Always having moved around in a troupe . . .

BROTHER SEBASTIAN

Yes, I see—so you just joined another?

BROTHER ANDREW

Why, the Abbot's not going to make me leave, is he?

BROTHER SEBASTIAN

No, I don't think so—not if you learn your conjugations silently, and let me try and finish this poem.

BROTHER ANDREW

Won't you read me a bit?

BROTHER SEBASTIAN

No, it needs polishing.

BROTHER ANDREW

I'll make allowances. Don't be shy.

BROTHER SEBASTIAN

Thank you. But you'll hear it later.

BROTHER ANDREW

I suppose you think I wouldn't understand it?

BROTHER SEBASTIAN

No, it wasn't that.
I'll tell you what I'll do: I'll read some if you stand down there and then you can tell me if you can hear it all right. The acoustics are a bit erratic; one's voice certainly goes up to heaven—
for nobody can hear you on earth.

BROTHER ANDREW (*going back*)

Here?

BROTHER SEBASTIAN

No, farther back. There, that'll do.
'Night that is darker than darkness,
  Night which no gentle evening
Leads in,
              nor dawn
                    alleviates,
nor sun penetrates;
                    night of no shadow;
Night . . .'

BROTHER ANDREW

Right, I'm ready.

BROTHER SEBASTIAN

But I've read it. Didn't you hear it?

BROTHER ANDREW

Not a word.

BROTHER SEBASTIAN

I'll have to stand farther from the statue.
I'll try again. . . .
'Night that is darker than darkness,
  Night which no gentle evening
Leads in,
              nor dawn
                    alleviates,
nor sun penetrates;
                    night of no shadow. . . .'
How's that?

BROTHER ANDREW

Not very good.

22

BROTHER SEBASTIAN

You mean the poem? Or can't you hear it?

BROTHER ANDREW

(*returning to him*)

You want to throw your voice. Look, like this:
And use your lips more and imagine you are talking
    to some person right at the back of the audience.

BROTHER SEBASTIAN

. . . You mean 'congregation'.

BROTHER ANDREW

YOU WANT TO SPEAK LIKE THIS,
or half the sound gets lost in the roof of the marquee . . .

BROTHER SEBASTIAN

. . . cathedral.

BROTHER ANDREW

But of course, it's easier if you've got a good house.

BROTHER SEBASTIAN

A what?

BROTHER ANDREW

If it's a good day . . . if the takings . . .
I mean, if you've got plenty of people in the tent . . .

BROTHER SEBASTIAN

Cathedral.

BROTHER ANDREW

Then the sound carries better, see?

BROTHER SEBASTIAN

Yes, I think we'll get a good house . . .
But I'll throw my voice as you showed me.
Thanks very much for the tip.

BROTHER ANDREW

That's all right—we artists have got to help each other, haven't
we?

BROTHER SEBASTIAN

Yes, that's true . . .
I wonder if you'd mind doing this sweeping for me while I
finish this poem?

BROTHER ANDREW
(taking the broom and sweeping)

Not at all,
I don't suppose I could help with the poem.

(Brother Gregory comes in carrying some roses)

BROTHER GREGORY

Brother Sebastian . . .

BROTHER SEBASTIAN

Yes, what is it now?

BROTHER GREGORY

As you're not doing anything, could you hold these flowers for
a moment while I get some water?

24

BROTHER SEBASTIAN
(*not looking up*)

Why, of course. I hate being idle.

BROTHER GREGORY
(*holding the flowers out*)

Well, come on then.
What are you doing now?

BROTHER SEBASTIAN

I'm just writing an inscription.
I've dedicated my poem to you.

BROTHER GREGORY

Really! I'm touched.

BROTHER SEBASTIAN

You will be (*reading it*): 'To my friend, Brother Gregory, with
   whose help this poem would never have been written.'
(*He goes to hold the flowers*)
And you needn't thrust the thorns into my hands quite so
   viciously.

BROTHER ANDREW
(*going to them, still holding his broom*)

Aren't they beautiful? (*pause*)
There's nothing like flowers, is there? (*pause*)
To cheer a place up, I mean.
Though, of course, they always remind me of funerals . . .
Do they remind you of funerals, Brother Sebastian?

BROTHER SEBASTIAN

Yes, that's why they cheer me up.

BROTHER ANDREW
(*coming closer*)

They are lovely.

BROTHER GREGORY

Do mind your broom . . .

BROTHER ANDREW

I'm sorry. Yes, they're the most beautiful roses I've ever seen.
They're almost too perfect, don't you think? (*pause*)
What's your favourite flower, Brother Sebastian? (*pause*)
I said: 'What's your favourite flower, Brother Sebastian?'

BROTHER SEBASTIAN

Black roses.

BROTHER ANDREW

Is it? How interesting!
Now, I've never seen a black rose.
Have you seen a black rose, Brother Gregory?

BROTHER GREGORY

They're all black at night.

BROTHER ANDREW

Are they now? How interesting.
But my favourite rose is a sweet brier rose.

BROTHER SEBASTIAN

Is it now?

26

BROTHER GREGORY

How interesting.

BROTHER ANDREW

Is it? Why, many people like the sweet-brier rose.
They're quite common in the hedges: indeed, they grow wild.
In fact I suppose they're not a rose at all.

BROTHER GREGORY

Not at all. They're a species of flowering thorn.

BROTHER ANDREW

How interesting. Still, they're very pretty . . .
But, of course, not as beautiful as yours—
Did you grow them all yourself?

BROTHER GREGORY

Nature took a hand here and there. (*He finishes arranging the
    flowers.*)
Now which is best—which is the most perfect rose of all?

BROTHER SEBASTIAN

What about this?

BROTHER GREGORY

No, it's a little too full.

BROTHER SEBASTIAN

Or this red one?

BROTHER GREGORY

Yes . . . or this white?
Now which of these two . . .?
It's very difficult.

BROTHER ANDREW

Why must you choose only one?

BROTHER GREGORY

To offer Our Lady the best, of course.

BROTHER ANDREW

Couldn't you give her all of them?

BROTHER GREGORY

No, her hands can only hold one rose;
And that must be the most perfect rose of all.

BROTHER ANDREW

Then let me help you.

BROTHER GREGORY
(*ignoring him*)

Now, shall it be the white or the red, Brother Sebastian?

BROTHER ANDREW
(*excitedly running up*)

The red! The red!

BROTHER GREGORY

Don't touch it!
Oh, now you've soiled it.

BROTHER ANDREW

I'm sorry. (*He returns to his sweeping.*)

BROTHER GREGORY

Now it will have to be the white!

BROTHER SEBASTIAN

No; choose the red.

BROTHER GREGORY

Why?

BROTHER SEBASTIAN

It's more appropriate. (*Brother Gregory places the red rose in a bowl to the left of the statue. Father Marcellus and Brother Justin come up the aisle.*)

FATHER MARCELLUS

The boys should, of course, lead the procession.
Now, show me where you want them to stand.

BROTHER JUSTIN

(*taking up a position to the left of the statue*)

Here, Father—when I rehearsed them yesterday,
I found that if they stood farther back,
Most of the sound got lost in the transepts.

FATHER MARCELLUS

Yes, yes, I know . . .

BROTHER GREGORY

But if the choir stand there, Brother Justin,
None of my flowers will be seen.

FATHER MARCELLUS

Is that the difficulty? Well, surely some compromise could put
    that right.
Let them stand forward, but more to the left.
If they're here, they will not hide the flowers—
Which reminds me, Brother Gregory, see that all the gardens
    are open to the villagers this evening.

BROTHER GREGORY

But . . .

FATHER MARCELLUS

Yes, I know we unaccountably lost all our pears last year;
But if you open the gates, the boys might get out of the habit of
    climbing the wall.
The flowers are beautiful. Have you chosen the rose?

BROTHER GREGORY

Yes, Father.

FATHER MARCELLUS

Then all is ready. And just in time.
Now the three of you should retire
And prepare yourselves for the ceremony. (*They turn to go.*)
And, Brother Justin, remember:
    your anthem should be heard and understood;
I cannot tolerate slovenly singing.
Tell your boys to bite their consonants as though they were an
    apple.
I'm sure Brother Sebastian agrees with me
—otherwise his lyric's wasted.

(*The three monks go. Father Marcellus examines the flowers. Brother
                Andrew is still sweeping.*)

30

BROTHER ANDREW

Father Abbot . . .

FATHER MARCELLUS

Yes, what is it?

BROTHER ANDREW

Isn't there anything I can do?

FATHER MARCELLUS

For what, my son?

BROTHER ANDREW

For her . . . I hear it's her birthday.
Nobody told me before,
Or I'd have done something special.

FATHER MARCELLUS

But you have! You've scrubbed the chapel . . .
I've never seen it so clean.

BROTHER ANDREW

Please, Father, isn't there anything I can do in the ceremony, I
    mean?

FATHER MARCELLUS

I'm afraid not, my son.

BROTHER ANDREW

Nothing?

FATHER MARCELLUS

No, you see, only three offerings are made each year;
And they are already chosen.
Besides, you can't write music or poetry, can you?

BROTHER ANDREW

No, but . . .

FATHER MARCELLUS

But what, my son?

BROTHER ANDREW

Couldn't I light the candles for her?

FATHER MARCELLUS

Why yes, of course. You light the candles.
Our Lady will be grateful for anything you can do.

BROTHER ANDREW

Anything, Father?

FATHER MARCELLUS

Of course.
And perhaps the more humble it is,
    the more she is pleased.
Yes, you light the candles, Brother Andrew.

BROTHER ANDREW

Thank you, Father. Shall I light them now?

FATHER MARCELLUS

No; wait until you see the procession coming up the aisle.

32

And don't forget to snuff them immediately the ceremony's
    over.
*(Father Marcellus goes off up the aisle, leaving Brother Andrew alone.
        Still holding his broom, he addresses the statue.)*

BROTHER ANDREW

I'm sorry. Nobody told me it was your birthday,
Or I'd have got you a present.
But I suppose it doesn't help to be told that now.
—Now it's too late to do anything about it?
But I'll make it up to you next year, you see if I don't.
I'll tell you what I'll do . . .
No, we'll keep it as a surprise, we will.
It's too late this year . . . isn't it? *(pause)*

If you'll excuse me, sweet Lady, I'll put the broom away and
    go and smarten myself up a bit.
Then I'll be right back to light your candles.
I shan't be a minute.

> *(Brother Andrew goes off, right.)*

ARIA *(tenor solo off)*

I tried to grasp it in words,
                    I failed.
Had I found it in words,
                        it would have been enough.
I tried to grasp it in song,
                    I failed.
Had I found it in song,
                        it would have been enough.
I tried to grasp it from love,
                    I failed:

Had I found it in love,

                     it would have been enough.

I tried to grasp it from Christ,

                     I succeeded.

Christ gave. I succeeded.

                     It is enough.

THE CELEBRATION OF THE FEAST DAY OF OUR LADY

Brother Andrew returns and lights the candles before the statue of the Virgin.

A choir of boys proceeds up the aisle in silence. It is followed by the three monks who are to make offerings; and lastly by the Abbot himself.

The full choir, which has remained in position, sings:

THE HYMN FOR A FESTIVAL

Now larks and linnets lift
Into the autumn sky,
And sing as though it's spring.
    Her day renews the year.

                Dies Mariae
                Mater Laudanda.

The fallen leaves fly up
On to the oak and beech,
And furl themselves again.
    Her life renews the year.

                Vita Mariae
                Mater Aeterna.

Frail blossom and firm fruit
Are seen upon one branch,

And daffodils return.
Her love renews the year.

Amor Mariae
Mater Amanda.

And where the stallion stamps
There, violets reappear
And all the earth is glad:
Her Son renews the year.

Puer Mariae
Mater Divina.

(*The boys' choir kneel at the left of the statue; the three monks on the steps before it. The Abbot ascends the pulpit and addresses the congregation.*)

FATHER MARCELLUS

Once again, my children, we have met to celebrate
The Feast Day of the Blessed Virgin.
Here, in this chapel which bears her name,
And before this statue made in Our Lady's likeness,
It is the custom of our ancient Order
to offer of our best
to her who gave the world its best.
As you all know, the Legend is:
That when the perfect offering is made,
This statue will move and make a sign.
Most of you will have witnessed this ceremony many
times.
Those of you who are old men saw it as young men.
And those of you who are here for the first time will be
children—
For no one in this part of the country
fails to celebrate the Feast Day of Our Lady.
All of you know that though we have made

These humble offerings so many times before:
  the statue has never moved.
And consequently some of you ask: how a statue made of stone
Can ever be expected to move. It is a reasonable question.
And I will answer it by asking you another question which is
  also reasonable.
It is this: Is it not more difficult for man
  To make a perfect offering out of his imperfect heart
  Than it is for a statue to move
  Though its muscles be of stone?
And not until that perfect offering is made
Can this legend be disproved.
When a miracle does not occur, it does not mean
That God has not the power to perform it,
But rather that we have not the virtue to deserve it,
Nor the faith to perceive it.
        Last year, as you will remember,
I chose three people from the village to make the offerings.
And so this year, as is our custom, I have given the privilege
To three brothers of this Order:
        Brother Sebastian has written a poem, Brother Justin
          has composed a song;
        and Brother Gregory, our gardener, has grown a rose.
Let us pray that Our Lady, the Blessed Virgin,
May graciously receive these humble offerings;
And that the imperfections of the gift
May be redeemed by the humility in which it is given.
(*The Abbot kneels, Brother Gregory rises and stands before the statue.*)

FATHER MARCELLUS

Laetabunda canant pie
Corda cuncta cor Mariae

36

Cor amandum omni corde,
Cor laudandum omni mente.

(The Abbot rises, Brother Gregory kneels.)

BROTHER GREGORY

Consors patris Dexterae
Fit Matris Deiparae
   Cor et natus

Flos cordis Altissimi
Flos cordis Virginei,
   Flos et fructus.

*(He rises and takes the rose from the altar. Then stands before the statue
again.)*

BROTHER GREGORY

Thou, who grew so pure
   On this earth,
That Jesus was thy flower
   At His Birth;

Thou, who stood alone
   At the cross,
And wept for thy own
   And the whole world's loss;

Thou, who saw their spears make scarlet flowers
   In His side,
Wounds which were His, yet scars that were ours
   As He died;

Now take this rose that was so white
   And is so red

Stained with the blood which from Him bled.
O Mary Mother,

> it was thy own they shed.

(He places the rose in the statue's hands, kneels for a second before it, then resumes his place on the steps beside the two other monks.)

FATHER MARCELLUS

What is there more fitting
Than that a rose should be given
  To her who is the Rose of all the world?
Yet Our Lady's statue did not move.
What imperfection can there be
In those frail petals which enclose
  All that grace which is a rose?
There can be none: for imperfection implies the potentialities
    of perfection.
Nothing is perfect unless it is immortal.
And, since everything in nature is material and mortal,
Nothing in nature is perfect.
Only man can be perfect;
For he alone has an immortal spirit.
Only man could be perfect.
Therefore it is he, alone, who is imperfect.

(The Abbot kneels, Brother Justin rises and stands before the statue.)

FATHER MARCELLUS

Cor aeterni numinis
En factum est Virginis
Cor aeternum.

(The Abbot rises, Brother Justin kneels.)

38

BROTHER JUSTIN

Haec est Virgo sapiens
Haec est Virgo rapiens
Cor divinum.

(He rises and conducts the choir of boys who sing his Anthem.)

ANTHEM TO THE VIRGIN

O Holy Mary
      who, for thy chastity,
Was chosen to bear
      Him whose birth was God's own birth,
Pray that He may forgive us our sin
As thou, in His infancy, comforted Him.

O Holy Mary
      who, for thy piety,
Was chosen to bear
      Him whose life gave grace to life,
Pray that we may be freed from our pride
As He, in humility, was at thy side.

O Holy Mary
      who, for thy purity,
Was chosen to bear
      Him whose death was death's own death,
Pray that He may grant us that rest
Which he, in His gentleness, gave to thy breast.

(Brother Justin turns and places his manuscript at the foot of the statue; then kneels for a moment before resuming his place on the steps. The choir also kneels.)

FATHER MARCELLUS

In music man reaches beyond his height

39

And makes a frail cathedral of sound,
A monument of a moment, transient
As himself.

It is an insubstantial edifice of order
Challenging the chaos of the night.

It is the spire of the human spirit.
Silence surrounds it, echo its answer.

Music is that sound to which a rose is shape.
Yet still the statue does not move.

Perhaps that is because nothing which delights our senses
Can be perfect.

For, since our senses are both mortal and imperfect,
That which delights them must be imperfect also.

(The Abbot kneels. Brother Sebastian rises and stands before the statue.)

FATHER MARCELLUS

Infundatur omnibus
Ros ille pectoribus
Accendatur cordibus
Flamma sacra.

(The Abbot rises, Brother Sebastian kneels.)

BROTHER SEBASTIAN

O Jesu cor Mariae
Ros, ignis, fons gratiae
Ure, purga, posside
Corda cuncta.

(He stands before the statue and delivers his canzone.)

40

As a small boy can
              run to his mother
and admit his naughtiness,
      certain of her forgiveness;
                  so are we
In all our ageless infancy
                able to come to thee,
Whose child was more than man,
                  making thou the Mother
Of us all. So now we can confess,
                  with childish artlessness,
                  To thee, O Holy Lady,
Who stood so lonely,
      and heard Him forgive that sin which was our sin,
           that pain which was His pain—though the agony

Was yours then, and must be now, since we deny Him
                            hourly;
And crucify Him daily:
                The Cross, the axle;
Humanity, the wheel,
                turning from birth to death,
Returning from death to birth,

While our circumference is sleep as we move from dream
                      to dream, and wearily
Wake to dream again. Only
                He, alone, is still
Beyond this mortal wheel
                which turns from birth to death;
Returns from death to birth.

O Holy Lady intercede for us
    that He may forgive us, not only those sins
Which we confess,
      but those we do not confess;
        not only those things we do against each other,
But those things we do not do for our Saviour,
                who was thy Son, O Holy Mother,
Intercede for us
    that He may grant us, not only that mercy
      which we seek,
        but that grace which we cannot even imagine;
Since we are chained to our own shadows,
      and our eyes are blind with our own sight,

As we stampede through the forest of our dreams, fleeing
From what we pursue; evading
    what we seek; always fearing to find
What is not lost, but lies within our mind;
      As a lake beneath the curtain of the night,
Sleeps concealed, till it is woken, and its surface broken,
              by the thirsty foal of light.

So is He within us. O Holy Mary, thy Son is waiting
Outside my empty heart, walking
    up and down my mind.
He stands as a beggar; yet it is I, who am blind.
      He does not seek for alms; but to give me sight;
For my eyes are blind with self-love, and all my days are night.

Night that is darker than darkness,
        night which no gentle evening
Leads in,
            nor dawn
                    alleviates,
Nor sun penetrates;
                    night of no shadow;
Night which is our loneliness,
                        loneliness of being,
Yet never living,—
                for to be comes after being born
            as does our death, so many times, so many years
            before the moment of our dying,
                    and in between our life's a state
Of loneliness which is not solitude; of being separate
    From Him, whose death we mourn, but to whom we are the
                                            sorrow.

Sorrow that is not anger, sorrow that falls
As summer rain falls,
            so lightly over,
So gently to cover
                field, thorn and flower. Then lies like a pearl
Of Joy, set in the crimson petal.

Joy that's a lark, joy that's a linnet, joy that falls
Out of the sky, a waterfall
                          of song for ever
Singing, and never
                    Silent. His joy is His love: both eternal.
It is we in our loneliness, who, in the crutch of the night,
        clutch ourselves to ourselves, and mourn for ourselves,
                                    who are mortal.

O Holy Mary,
      only Virgin
To be mother;
        the only mother,
              out of all the labour
In all the world,
        to see a son die, yet rise from the dead.
O Holy Mary,
      only Virgin
To be mother;
        yet there is no Mother
Who does not weep with your tears,
        who does not pray with your words. Intercede

For them, for us, that our sin of self-love may be forgiven;
That we be not forsaken;
          Pray through His compassion
We may partake of His Resurrection;
     O Holy Mother, with thy prayers and His pity, even
Man might live, and death might die,
            Through Jesus Christ, *Amen.*

(He places his manuscript at the foot of the statue, then kneels before it
  before resuming his place beside the other two monks on the steps.)

45

Where music failed how could poetry succeed,
When it is lamed with words,
Words that are worn with our complaint.
And all our complaint is pride.
    Perhaps poetry lies only in pity
    And perhaps the spirit is articulate only in its tears.
The statue has made no sign; and that is just.
For we cannot expect to move God by our achievements;
It is only when man is humble
That he is worthy of God's pride.
    Let us pray that Our Lady, the Blessed Virgin,
Who has graciously received these offerings,
May intercede for us who are not worthy. (*He kneels.*)

Amor, Amor, Amor propera,
Ubique imperia
    In terris ut super sidera.

(*He rises and leads the Recession down the aisle to the accompaniment of the 'Hymn for a Festival' sung by the full choir. Only Brother Andrew is left. He snuffs the candles. Then turns and looks down the church to make sure he is alone and unobserved. Then, while the following song is sung (off), Brother Andrew removes his habit to reveal a clown's smock beneath.*)

ARIA (*tenor solo off.*)
Love that is passion
And all compulsion
        devours me.

Love that is treason,
Betraying reason,
        deceives me.

Love that is mercy,
Tender as Mary,
                              evades me.

Love that is gracious,
Gentle as Jesus,
                              awaits me.

*(Brother Andrew, now dressed as a clown, kneels before the statue of
the Virgin.)*

BROTHER ANDREW

Ave Maria, Gratia Plena,
Dominus tecum, Benedicta tu in mulieris . . .
I mean, 'in mulieres', no, 'in mulierorum'
Dear me, that's not right either . . .
You see, I cannot even pray to you as the others do.
Though I've learned your prayers by heart,
They will not stay within my head,
But come and go, in one ear and out the other
With nothing to stay them in between.
The only phrase I know
Is 'quia amore langueo'—
Anyhow, Latin's no language to talk to a young woman in—
    begging your pardon, O Holy Mother. . . .
                              (He rises.)

Sweet Lady, I mean no disrespect;
You see me as I am.
I put this on especially for you.
It's five years if it's a day since I wore them—
But I daresay you've guessed all along
    that they call me Brother Andrew
Only because I was once Merry Andrew,

the circus clown, juggler and tumbler
known half the world over—
   well, in this part of the country.
And now that we're alone, I've a surprise for you,
A special treat for your Feast Day.
Father Marcellus told me himself only this morning
That you, in your graciousness, would receive
   any offering I made, however humble.
I can't write poetry, nor compose a song
(never having had much time for either)
But tumble, juggle and vault I can do
(though self-praise is no recommendation
   as we say in the Ring).
I can stand on my head till the cows come home.
I can balance a chair on the end of my nose.
As for juggling, I can keep five balls in the air
   with one hand tied behind me back
(though between you and me there's nothing to it,
merely a knack and ten years' practice).
   But it was for the Roman vault
that I used to be called again and again.
I can do the Roman vault, the Spanish vault
and the French double turn.
I can somersault forwards.
I can somersault backwards
   and clap me hands in mid-air
   and land where I left the ground.
All this I'll do for you.
It'll be your own Gala Performance,
'By Special Command', as they say.
I hope you like it, for there's nothing else I can do.
And O Sweet Lady, how I love you,
   After my own fashion, how I love you.

Though others may worship you with words,
See, Mary, I adore you with my heart
                    and with my hands
                              and with my feet.
(He begins to tumble energetically but clumsily. The more he tries, the more he fails. He attempts every kind of somersault and botches each. Finally, he kneels, breathless and dishevelled, before the statue.)

I'm sorry. It wasn't very good, was it?
Don't tell me. I know. It was terrible, terrible.
I messed up every one.
Some acrobat—as agile and awkward as a rheumatic crab.
It's only that I'm out of practice.
Yes, see how breathless I am.
Not so young as I was—getting old. . . .
And an old clown's as useless as an old egg.
    I suppose that's how it always is:
When we at last find someone worth loving,
We've nothing left worth offering. *(He stands.)*

But I have it!
I know what I can still do for you:
I can do my Pierrot's Dance.
I used to do it while they were fixing up the cage
    for the man-eating lions. . . .
It used to go over quite well. . . .
It's rather a sad dance—but I know you'll understand it;
Sadness comes as easy to a clown as it did to the Mother of
    Jesus (meaning no offence, of course).
Yes, I'm sure you'll like it . . .
It is slow and graceful. . . . *(He begins to dance.)*

D   *49*

Or it's meant to be.
I made it all up myself.

Let me see now: one, two and three; one, two and three,
One 'pas de chat', one 'battement';
Now a 'pirouette'—no, that comes later. . . .

(He stops and begins a second time.)

One, two and three; one, two and three. . . .
As you see, it's not a Pavane,
And it's not a Chaconne;
But slower that the first, and more graceful than either—
or meant to be.

I made it all up myself.
It's all about a man who fell in love with a lady who
was beyond his reach.
I suppose he was a dwarf and she was very tall.
So the poor little man courted her by standing on
his toes. . . .
(ah, that's where the pirouette comes in)
and, having deceived his Lady this way,
the poor little man had to go on walking on his
toes. . . doing everything on his toes.
And, as his toes got tireder and tireder,
he sank smaller and smaller. . . .

(He overbalances.)
Sorry, I haven't got the time quite right
Yes, I'm sure the tempo used to be steadier. . . .
One, two and three; one, two and three.
As I was saying:
As the little man got older and older,
he got smaller and smaller. . . .

That was meant for a full pirouette
But I lost my balance. . . .

And as the little man got older and smaller,
the higher he had to stand on his toes
which got tireder and tireder,
so he had to jump and spring into the air.
(He tries a tour en l'air.)
Yes, that's where I did a 'tour en l'air'. . . .
Wait, I'll try it again.
(He goes across to repeat the step.)
And the tireder and smaller the little man got,
the more his lady seemed beyond his reach;
as his shoulders were bent and his legs were doubled
I'm sure the tempo used to be steadier. . . .
*(He goes across to repeat the step almost
sobbing the lines which precede it.)*
And the tireder and smaller the little man got
the more his lady seemed beyond his reach
as he sank down on his knees.
(He ends clumsily.)
No use, I can't do it! I can't do it!
(He goes to the statue.)
That's the worst of fairy stories.
They always come true,
especially when you make them up yourself.
(He kneels to the statue.)
Sweet Lady, forgive me.
Treat me not with utter contempt.
Oh the pity I had not you to dance to
when I was young enough to dance.
Then I would have had all the grace in all the world.
But now, there is nothing I can do.

And here am I, sorry for myself,
When I should be sorry for you—
For it's your birthday, isn't it. And now you're
                                    disappointed,
And look like a child looks when nobody has come to her
                                    party.

No, we can't leave things like that, can we?
Merry Andrew won't give in yet; he'll cheer you up
And bring not only a smile to your lips—
  (for that's easy)
He'll make you laugh with your eyes;
  and that's difficult, especially for your eyes.
Though I can't tumble or dance, I can sing!
I'll tell you what I'll do:
I'll sing you a little song which used to make the children
                                    laugh.
It's all about your feast day, so I hope you won't take
                                    offence.
I made it all up myself—and it rimes, too
(though, of course, I don't pretend to be no poet.)
It's called 'Poor Old Me'.
  (*He begins to croak the following ballad, holding his knee.*)
    On the Feast of Our Lady, I'd hurt my poor knee;
      Ah me, I'd hurt my poor knee.
    On the Feast of Our Lady, I'd hurt my poor knee
    On a gate,—what a penance a bruised knee can be!
          (*He turns to the statue to emphasize his rime.*)
    Good Saint Peter, come and put a poultice on
    Poor old me.
    So I stood on my feet to pray.

    On the Feast of Our Lady, I'd hurt my poor foot,
                              (*He clutches it.*)

Ah me, I'd hurt my poor foot.
On the Feast of Our Lady, I'd hurt my poor foot
On a rock,—and the swelling split open my boot!
(*He almost nudges the statue lest his rime be missed.*)
Mary, aid me!
Good Saint Peter come and put a poultice on
Poor old me!
So I lay on my back to pray. (*He does so.*)

On the Feast of Our Lady, I'd hurt my poor back;
Ah me, I'd hurt my poor back.
On the Feast of Our Lady, I'd hurt my poor back
With a log. And I felt I'd been laid on the wrack.
Father Abraham, Isaac and Esau.
Mary, aid me!
Good Saint Peter, come and put a poultice on
Poor old me.
So I knelt on my shoulders to pray.
(*He arches his back.*)
On the Feast of Our Lady, I'd hurt my poor shoulder;
Ah me, I'd hurt my poor shoulder.
On the Feast of Our Lady, I'd hurt my poor shoulder
At work. That's a serious thing when you're older!
(*He raises a foot to emphasize his double rime.*)
Bell, book and candle, incense, water!
Father Abraham, Isaac and Esau.
Mary, aid me.
Good Saint Peter, come and put a poultice on
Poor old me!
So I stood on my head to pray!
(*He attempts this position.*)
On the Feast of Our Lady, I'd hurt my poor head;
Ah me, I'd hurt my poor head.

53

On the Feast of Our Lady, I'd hurt my poor head
On a beam. May Our Lady forgive what I said!
   Mary, aid me . . . no, that's not right. . . .
         (*He realizes he's got muddled and starts shouting wildly.*)
   Bell, book and candle, incense, water!
   Good Saint Peter. . . . No, that comes after . . .
                  (*He tries to catch up with the music.*)
   Isaac, Esau, Father Abraham!
Wait, Wait, Oh, don't go away!
         (*Still standing on his head, he tries to remember the words
         whilst the accompaniment continues. . . . Slowly, he gets
         to his feet.*)
I've forgotten it!
O sweet Lady, is there nothing I can do
   to show my love for you? Nothing? Nothing?
I can't pray. I can't dance. I can't sing.
I can't even somersault. Can't I?
         (*He now throws himself violently and hysterically about,
         trying to somersault. The accompaniment gets quicker and
         quicker.*)
Watch, watch . . . this time. . . .
         (*He crashes against the altar but picks himself up to try
         again. The noise brings in Father Marcellus and the
         three monks. The music ceases.*)

BROTHER SEBASTIAN

What's that noise?

BROTHER JUSTIN

Look!

BROTHER GREGORY

Quick! Stop him! Stop him!
   (*They rush up the aisle while he continues to hurl himself about. The
   music starts again.*)

BROTHER ANDREW

When Merry Andrew can no longer tumble
What's the use of Merry Andrew eh?
This time, I'll do it, or . . . or . . .
I'll curl myself into a ball
And throw myself away. (*He takes a run in silence.*)

BROTHER SEBASTIAN

It's sacrilege! Stop him! Stop him!
Brother Andrew . . .
(*Brother Sebastian goes to stop the clown but the Abbot prevents him.*)

FATHER MARCELLUS

No, let him try again.
He offers all he has, and with what humility.

BROTHER ANDREW
(*taking another run in silence*)

See, Mary, I adore you with my heart
    and with my hands
      and with my feet. . . .

FATHER MARCELLUS

No, leave him.
Who are we to say how God would have us worship.
He tries for her sake and not his own sake.
(*Now the clown makes a final, violent effort and falls at the foot of the
statue. He is broken.*)

BROTHER ANDREW

Sweet Lady, I can never reach thee

Unless thou reach down to lift me. . . .
Quia amore langueo.

> (*He collapses. Brother Sebastian goes to him.*)

FATHER MARCELLUS
(*as if to himself*)

Seek not to embrace Me
But rather that I should embrace thee.

BROTHER SEBASTIAN

He is dead.

> (*The statue of the Virgin drops the rose upon the body. The monks kneel.
> The full choir begins to sing the 'Hymn for the Dead'.*)

FATHER MARCELLUS
(*He goes to the body and takes the rose.*)

Rose of pity, flower of passion,
Bleeds for ever, petals crimson;
Rose of Mary, Christ's compassion.

> (*he places the rose on a white cushion and stands before the statue.*)

Stabat Mater dolorosa
Juxta crucem lacrymosa
Dum pendebat Filius
Cujus animam gementem
Contristatam et dolentem,
Pertransivit gladius.

> (*he returns to the body.*)

O Holy Mary, Virgin Mother,
Is there no way for love to enter
A man's small heart
Unless he first breaks that heart?

> (*the monks rise and lift the body. Father Marcellus turns again to
> the statue.*)

56

Eja Mater, fons amoris
Me sentire vim doloris
Fac, ut tacem lugeam
Fac, ut ardeat cor meum
In amando Christum Deum
Ut sibi complaceam.

(the monks begin to bear the body down the aisle. The Abbot follows,
carrying the rose. The choir continue to sing the Hymn.)

HYMN FOR THE DEAD

Hour of mourning, day of sorrow;
See the river drags a shadow:
Velvet grief and hollow echo.

Close his eyes and bring clean linen;
Bear this body which is broken;
Let these obsequies be spoken.

All that dances, dances to us;
All that's growing, grows towards us;
All that's chaste, is wanton with us.

Heloise found us her lover;
Lovely Helen we embroider;
Flesh our fabric, we the weaver.

Nothing's born, but we're born with it;
Nothing lives, but we live on it;
Nothing dies, but we devour it.

Every battle is our conquest;
Pestilence and plague our harvest;
We the termites in death's forest.

As a leper in the gutter,
See his shadow stalks its master:
Phantom sentry, lonely mourner.

Now his dreams like wolves are baying
Over him, beyond all dreaming,
Since in death there's no desiring.

Death embraces all that's vital;
Death is jealous of Death's rival;
Death is endless, Christ's eternal.

Wake this man whom Death has taken;
Take this heart which life has broken;
Break this web which Death has woven.

May he rest, not be forgotten;
May he sleep and yet be woken;
May his faith be not forsaken.

Rose of pity, flower of passion,
Bleeds for ever, petals crimson;
Rose of Mary, Christ's compassion.

May the gentle earth enclose him;
And the wind and rain embalm him,
Till the day when Christ redeems him.

Virgin Mary, Holy Mother,
Intercede with God our Father,
To receive his soul for ever.

Amen.

Ensi fina li menestrex:
Buer i tuma, buer i servi,
Car haute honor i deservi,
A cui nule ne se compere.
Ce nos racontent li saint pere
Qu'ensi avint ce menestrel.
Or prions Deu, il n'i a tel,
Qu'il nos doinst lui bien servir,
Que s'amor puissons deservir.
Explicit del Tumeor.